CAPTURED
SCIENCE
HISTORY

FUKUSHIMA DISASTER

HOW A TSUNAMI UNLEASHED NUCLEAR DESTRUCTION

by Danielle Smith-Llera

Content Adviser: Michael Wert, PhD
Associate Professor of History
Marquette University

COMPASS POINT BOOKS
a capstone imprint

Compass Point Books are published by Capstone,
1710 Roe Crest Drive, North Mankato, Minnesota 56003
www.mycapstone.com

Editor: Catherine Neitge
Designer: Catherine Neitge
Media Researcher: Svetlana Zhurkin
Library Consultant: Kathleen Baxter
Production Specialist: Laura Manthe

Scientific Adviser: Frank Summers, PhD, Outreach Astrophysicist,
Space Telescope Science Institute

Image Credits
DVIC: NARA, 19, 20, 23, 57 (top); Getty Images: Keystone, 34; Library of Congress,
21, 56; Newscom: Abaca USA/Air Photo Service, 39, 59, Abaca/GeoEye, 5, AFLO/
Rodrigo Reyes Marin, 52, Glasshouse Images, 32, Kyodo, 27, 35, 49, 50, 55, 58
(bottom), MCT/Staff, 10, Polaris/Hitoshi Katanoda, 46, Reuters/Issei Kato, 43,
Reuters/Kim Kyung-Hoon, cover, 13, 17, 45, Reuters/Kyodo, 8, 11, Reuters/Reuters
TV, 42, Reuters/Yomiuri, 12, Reuters/Yuriko Nakao, 15, World History Archive, 31;
Reuters, 40; Shutterstock: Eight Photo, 37, 58 (top), Everett Historical, 24, OBJM, 7,
TasfotoNL, 29; Wikimedia: U.S. Department of Energy, 57 (bottom)

Library of Congress Cataloging-in-Publication Data

Names: Smith-Llera, Danielle, 1971– author.
Title: Fukushima disaster : how a tsunami unleashed nuclear destruction / by
Danielle Smith-Llera.
Description: North Mankato, Minnesota : Capstone Press, [2018] | Series: CPB grades
4-8. Captured science history | Audience: Age 10-14. | Includes bibliographical
references and index.
Identifiers: LCCN 2017037864 (print) | LCCN 2017038534 (ebook) |
ISBN 9780756557508 (eBook PDF) | ISBN 9780756557423 (hardcover) |
ISBN 9780756557461 (paperback)
Subjects: LCSH: Fukushima Nuclear Disaster, Japan, 2011—Juvenile literature. |
Nuclear accidents—Japan—Fukushima-ken—Juvenile literature. | Environmental
disasters—Japan—Fukushima-ken—Juvenile literature.
Classification: LCC TK1365.J3 (ebook) | LCC TK1365.J3 S65 2018 (print) | DDC
363.17/990952117—dc23
LC record available at https://lccn.loc.gov/2017037864

Printed in Canada.
010798S18

TABLEOFCONTENTS

ChapterOne
DANGEROUS WAVES

Atsufumi Yoshizawa was just finishing his shift at Japan's Fukushima Daiichi nuclear plant. Two seawalls stretched into the Pacific Ocean like arms protecting the collection of turquoise-blue and white buildings. Yoshizawa, a nuclear engineer, helped run the plant, which produced electricity for millions of customers, including people in Tokyo, 177 miles (285 kilometers) away. It was a relaxed Friday afternoon, March 11, 2011. But the seafloor was restless.

The bottom of the sea is part of Earth's crust, which is made of massive plates that fit loosely together like puzzle pieces. They usually slide past each other about as slowly as fingernails grow. But off the eastern coast of Japan, along a crack in the crust called a fault, the edges of two plates pushed against each other, locked in battle.

No one at Fukushima Daiichi was aware of the struggling undersea plates on March 11. It was business as usual at the plant. Since the 1880s many electrical plants have burned coal to make steam power to generate electricity. But nuclear plants use another method—they split the smallest pieces of matter, atoms, to make heat. When an atom's nucleus splits, it releases energy in waves, most in the form of heat. Many types of atoms can produce abundant nuclear energy. This

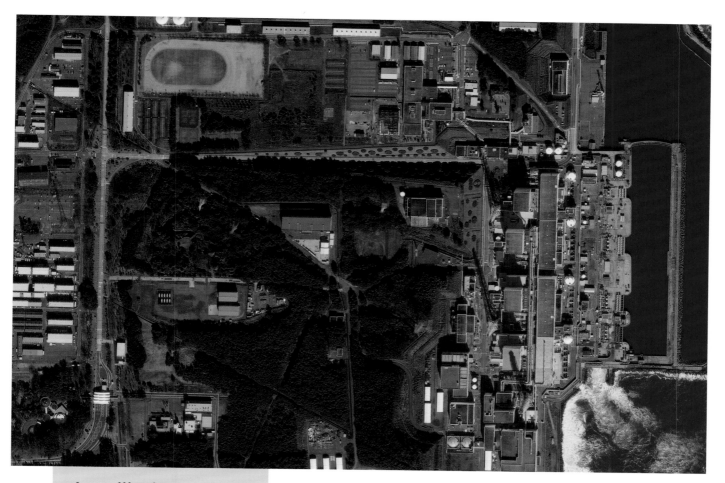

A satellite image of the Fukushima Daiichi nuclear plant was taken before disaster struck.

process is called fission. It is safe, as long as people are protected from its intense heat and dangerous radiation. The Fukushima nuclear plant housed six huge containers, called reactor vessels. Each was about six stories high, with walls made of steel 5 inches (13 centimeters) thick, plus concrete. Each reactor held thousands of fuel rods made of uranium, a silvery metal made of atoms that split easily.

On this Friday afternoon, as Yoshizawa walked down a plant corridor, tremendous energy was about to be released—but not inside the plant's reactors.

At 2:46 p.m., about 80 miles (129 km) off the coast, the seafloor rose violently. It was the epicenter of an earthquake.

Japan experiences more than 2,000 earthquakes a year, ranging from weak tremors to quakes that sway buildings. Sensors detect the traveling waves of motion and send warnings to TV and radio stations and cellphones. Students duck under desks, surgeons pause operations, and high-speed trains stop.

But Yoshizawa knew this earthquake was different. He fell to his hands and knees as the building swayed and ceiling panels crashed down. "I managed to look out of a window and saw parked cars bouncing up and down from the sheer force of the earthquake," he said. "I had never experienced anything like it." It lasted five or six minutes. The magnitude 9.0 earthquake was one of the strongest ever recorded. Thousands of miles away, it caused water to slosh in Norway's fjords and ice in Antarctica to crack. It shoved Japan about 8 feet (2.4 meters) east, and it even changed the way Earth spins.

Sensors at the plant triggered the automatic shutdown of fission inside Fukushima Daiichi's three active reactors, units 1, 2, and 3. When the earthquake cut off electricity to the plant, generators switched on to keep lights and equipment running. Yoshizawa joined manager Masao Yoshida in the plant's earthquake-proof bunker. They determined that the

"I managed to look out of a window and saw parked cars bouncing up and down from the sheer force of the earthquake."

The devastating tsunami that followed the magnitude 9.0 earthquake carried boats far inland.

plant's employees were safe, and the 40-year-old plant was undamaged.

But the jolting plates had disturbed the ocean. Large waves were traveling away from the epicenter of the earthquake. They approached Japan's coast at 100 mph (160 kph). Almost an hour after the earthquake, they surged up to 6 miles (10 km) inland. Former Fukushima resident Ryo Kanouya remembered the "soup of seawater, cars, houses, and everything the tsunami carried." The waves flooded 216 square miles (560 square km), killing almost 20,000 people. Inside the windowless bunker, Yoshizawa heard reports of the destruction and

"couldn't imagine a tsunami that big," he said later. The plant's designers hadn't imagined it either. To withstand earthquakes, they had built Fukushima Daiichi on solid rock. But when crews dug away 27 yards (25 m) of soil before construction, they put the plant within easy reach of tsunami waves. At 3:42 p.m., the first of seven waves struck the plant. One was more than 50 feet (15 m) high, more than twice the height of the plant's seawalls.

Lights went out and machines went silent. Tsunami waves had flooded basements, destroying generators and electrical circuits. Plant engineer

Takeyuki Inagaki later remembered "a terrifying situation. And the operators weren't sure what was happening. We couldn't even tell if there was water in the nuclear reactors." Water did not belong around the plant's electronics. Yet it was essential inside reactors.

Electric pumps normally circulate water through the reactor containers to keep fuel rods from overheating. Even after fission is shut down, hot fuel rods need up to 24 hours to cool. Without working pumps to replace water that's boiling away to steam, fuel rods heat so much that they can melt together. This molten mass can burn through the protective container, releasing life-threatening radiation into the air. Meltdown is a nuclear plant worker's nightmare.

Rushing around the dark control room with flashlights, workers shared a single concern: Were the fuel rods safe? Without working gauges, no one knew.

Plant manager Yoshida scrambled to make a plan. "What was happening was beyond what we trained for on a daily basis," a plant worker later explained. He called it "a race against time." Workers collected car batteries to hook up to gauges. Around 9 p.m., instruments came weakly to life—with alarming news. The water level inside unit 1, normally 20 feet (6 m) above the fuel rods, had dropped to just inches. Meanwhile, pressure soared as steam and gas filled the reactor vessel. Unit 1 was a time bomb.

Yoshida planned to relieve the pressure the way

a whistling teapot releases steam—through a small opening. Winds would carry radioactive steam over towns. But an explosion inside the reactor vessel would release far more radiation. Japan's prime minister, Naoto Kan, ordered anyone living within 6 miles (10 km) of the plant to evacuate. People abandoned their search for loved ones in the tsunami-wrecked zone to flee a wave of radiation.

Venting the reactor vessel is easy—if the plant has electricity. Workers simply open valves remotely from the control room. On Saturday morning, workers wearing gas masks and head-to-toe protective suits entered the reactor building to open valves by hand. Yoshida feared that his men were a "suicide squad." Their dosimeters, machines to measure radiation, registered shockingly high radiation levels. Workers struggled with a valve, and by midafternoon steam leaked from unit 1's exhaust tower.

Just an hour later, relief turned to panic. As the container's heat spiked to 5,072 degrees Fahrenheit (2,800 degrees Celsius), more than half the surface temperature of the sun, the zirconium coating around the uranium had produced explosive hydrogen gas.

Twenty-four hours earlier, TV screens had broadcast video of dark seawater destroying the coast. Now TV viewers watched the explosion at unit 1. Among them were Japan-based photojournalists who shoot images of unfolding news

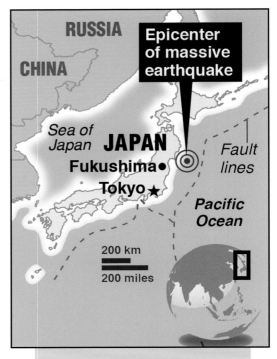

The epicenter of the earthquake was 80 miles (129 km) off the east coast of Japan.

AN INVISIBLE ENEMY

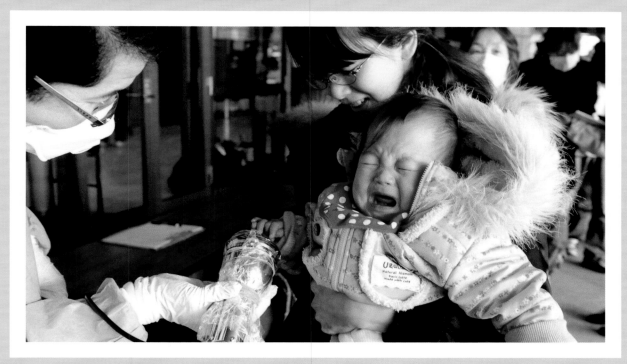

A baby and her mother were scanned for radiation at a Fukushima evacuation center in March 2011.

Cameras captured frightening explosions in Fukushima Daiichi, but not the greatest danger. "We were fighting an invisible enemy—out-of-control reactors," engineer Takeyuki Inagaki remembered later. "It was like fighting a war." Radiation absorbed by human tissue is measured in units called sieverts. Most people are exposed to natural radiation of 2 or 3 millisieverts (mSv) a year. On March 15 Fukushima Daiichi released its highest level of radiation: 400 mSv per hour. That is 20 times the annual exposure for uranium miners and employees in the nuclear industry.

Radiation, in the form of visible light, heat, microwaves, and radio waves, moves through the air as harmless waves. But the radiation inside a nuclear reactor is dangerous. It is released by new elements that are created by fission during chain reactions. Certain elements are unstable because they hold too much energy. The excess energy radiates into the air.

Radiation waves can pass through the skin. Radiation can also get into people's mouths or lungs. Once inside the body, radiation damages living cells and destroys the genetic information inside them. A single high dose can cause vomiting, hair loss, and bleeding gums. But even small doses can cause cancer because radiation collects in the body.

A community-run lab about 40 miles (60 km) from the Fukushima plant tracks radiation levels in soil, water, and food. "In universities, data is handled by qualified students, who have taken exams qualifying them to measure radiation. Here it's done by mothers working part-time. It's a crazy situation," said Kaori Suzuki, director of Tarachine, the nonprofit organization that runs the lab. "As ordinary citizens we had no knowledge about radiation at all. All we knew was that it is frightening," Suzuki said. "We can't see, smell, or feel radiation levels. Given this invisibility, it was extremely difficult for us. How do we fight it? The only way is to measure it."

Houses that were swept out to sea by the devastating tsunami burned out of control in northeastern Japan.

events as a profession. "I have covered many disasters and incidents over the last 10 years, but these things had little direct effect on my life," said Kim Kyung-Hoon, a Reuters news agency photographer. "By and large, those catastrophes had nothing to do with my personal life. Once my assignment was over, I used to go back to my normal life and switch from emergency mode." But the Fukushima story was different. "I am not exempt from the fear caused by

Kim Kyung-Hoon photographed police officers wearing protective suits as they searched for bodies.

the disaster," he said, "nor am I immune to the threat of the invisible nuclear radiation."

Miraculously, there was also good news: Hydrogen had escaped into unit 1's building and blown up its roof, not its reactor container. Lower pressure inside the reactor meant cooling water could now be forced inside. With the plant's freshwater stores empty, Yoshida turned to the Pacific Ocean's endless supply. Firefighters rushed through high radiation to lay hoses between the ocean and the plant. By 7:04 p.m., seawater was spraying into unit 1's reactor vessel.

Then a startling message came from the plant's owners. Tokyo Electric and Power Company (TEPCO) ordered the seawater spraying to stop because saltwater would destroy the reactor. But Yoshida defied them. As TEPCO monitored the bunker with video cameras, Yoshida commanded his workers to stop spraying, but he whispered for them to continue. Yoshida later said that "suspending the seawater could have meant death" for those at the plant.

Like tsunami waves, one disaster followed another. The next day, Sunday, March 13, workers struggled to vent unit 3 as water levels dropped and pressure rose. With dismay, they discovered that the valve had no handles. The day after that, an explosion rocked unit 3 and injured 11 workers. Meanwhile, unit 2 was in trouble too. Engineer Takeyuki Inagaki recalled that Yoshida "begged us to again go to the field to save unit 2."

Tuesday morning, March 15, began with a third explosion. Shockingly, it was in unit 4. How could it have exploded if it had been inactive when the tsunami hit? Near the top of each reactor vessel, deep pools held hundreds of used fuel rods because they remain radioactive for years. Had they overheated and evaporated the water? Workers panicked. The rods could ignite into a massive radioactive fire.

Millions of people, including the population of Tokyo, would have to be evacuated. Prime Minister Kan later said he had "feared the entire nation of Japan would be paralyzed by chaos."

On this stressful day, most workers fled the plant. Government authorities had already ordered people living within 12 miles (20 km) of the nuclear plant to evacuate. A small group of TEPCO workers, later known as the Fukushima 50, stayed behind. The group at the plant, which included more than 60 men, slept on the floor, surviving on biscuits and rationed water. "I never thought of leaving," recalled nuclear

Fukushima residents crowded into a school gym after they were forced to leave their homes near the plant.

engineer Atsufumi Yoshizawa. "We knew that we would not be replaced. No one was forced to stay, but those of us who remained knew that we would be there until the end. We knew that we were the only people capable of saving the plant. Our determination surpassed all other considerations." Yoshida asked them to sign their names on a board as "a record of the men who stayed to fight to the end."

Then unit 3's storage pool seemed to be boiling away too. On Thursday, March 17, helicopters buzzed over dumping water, but little reached the target. A day later, firefighters hustled through high radiation levels to position fire trucks. Soon precise arcs of seawater gushed into storage pools. Finally "we started to have some hope," recalled Inagaki. By March 22, repair work had allowed electricity to reach Fukushima Daiichi's reactors. By December temperatures inside them dropped below boiling. But Yoshida grimly reminded plant workers, "You still have a difficult road ahead."

The tsunami set off disasters that interrupted or ended lives. An investigation in 2012 by the Japanese Parliament concluded that the nuclear accident "was clearly man-made." But how, if no one could have stopped the earthquake or the tsunami waves?

Japanese officials wore protective gear in the aftermath of the Fukushima Daiichi nuclear plant disaster.

ChapterTwo
UNLOCKING THE ATOM

Sixty-six years before the 2011 tsunami, Japanese people searched for survivors in the wrecked city of Hiroshima. At 8:16 a.m. on August 6, 1945, a force as powerful as 15,000 tons (13,610 metric tons) of the explosive TNT hit the city. It was not an earthquake or any natural disaster. It was an atomic bomb dropped by a U.S. B-29 bomber. The explosion and its immediate effects killed more than 80,000 people.

The bomb was designed to unleash heat and power with nuclear fission. Survivor Shinji Mikamo, who was working on a roof, later remembered suddenly "facing a gigantic fireball. It was at least five times bigger and 10 times brighter than the sun. … The deafening noise came next. I was surrounded by the loudest thunder I had ever heard. It was the sound of the universe exploding." Its force tore open bodies. Its heat burned skin away. Survivor Sunao Tsuboi remembered that people "looked like ghosts, bleeding and trying to walk before collapsing." Many of those who survived the blast were sickened, and many died days and even years later. Today about 140,000 deaths are blamed on the bomb.

U.S. President Harry Truman believed atomic weapons would end World War II by forcing Japan to surrender, as its ally Nazi Germany had

An atomic bomb hit Nagasaki on August 9, 1945.

done three months earlier. After the United States dropped a second atomic bomb, on Nagasaki, Japan surrendered. Radios across Japan carried Emperor

Battered statues stood among the rubble after the bombing of Nagasaki, Japan, in 1945.

Hirohito's voice: "The enemy has begun to employ a new and most cruel bomb, the power of which to do damage is, indeed, incalculable, taking the toll of many innocent lives. Should we continue to fight, it would not only result in an ultimate collapse and obliteration of the Japanese nation, but also it would lead to the total extinction of human civilization."

Six years earlier, German-born physicist Albert Einstein had predicted the creation of an atomic bomb. As World War II began, Einstein worried that the Nazis would discover how to make nuclear weapons. After all, many of the world's scientists knew enough about

Albert Einstein became a U.S. citizen in 1940.

atoms to do it. Einstein had proposed a theory that the mass of objects can change into energy. Could this idea apply to the tiny atom?

Scientists knew that an atom's electrons revolve continuously. Protons and neutrons are bound tightly in a central cluster called the nucleus. Nuclear energy is so strong that the atom had been named using the Greek term for "indivisible." But in 1936, Danish physicist Niels Bohr proposed a revolutionary idea— the atom's nucleus could behave like a drop of liquid, changing shape, and even splitting.

In December 1938 German chemists Otto Hahn and Fritz Strassmann demonstrated in Berlin that a uranium atom could be split. When they bombarded uranium atoms with neutrons, they found an astonishing result—heavy uranium atoms broke into atoms with fewer protons in their nuclei, forming new, lighter elements. Nuclear fission had taken place. Their colleague, Austrian physicist Lise Meitner, confirmed it mathematically.

Some scientists found this discovery frightening. Once it started, fission could quickly get out of control. When an atom splits, it releases not only heat, but neutrons. The neutrons slam into other atoms, causing them to split and release more energy and more neutrons in an ongoing process. Hungarian physicist Leó Szilárd, who fled to the United States to escape the Nazis, convinced his friend Einstein of the danger. On August 2, 1939, Einstein signed an urgent letter to President Franklin Roosevelt warning him that it seemed "almost certain" that it would be "possible to set up a nuclear chain reaction in a large mass of uranium, by which vast amounts of power and large quantities of new radium-like elements would be generated." The letter said it "would also lead to the construction of bombs, and it is conceivable—though much less certain—that extremely powerful bombs of a new type may thus be constructed." The Einstein letter also pointed out that the Nazis appeared to be hoarding uranium. Nuclear fission had been discovered in Berlin. Would the world's first atomic bomb be built by the Germans?

Before that question was answered, Germany invaded European countries. Japan began invading Asian countries. On September 27, 1940, Japan signed a pact with Germany and Italy that became known as the Axis alliance. But the United States was still reluctant to join the fight in faraway Europe and Asia.

Then Japan gave the United States no choice. On the morning of December 7, 1941, more than 350 low-flying planes approached the U.S. Navy base at Hawaii's Pearl Harbor. "There are red circles on those planes overhead. They are Japanese!" a witness cried. For 90 minutes, U.S. soldiers, sailors, airmen, and Marines scrambled in confusion as Japanese bombs tore into U.S. military ships and airplanes. About

Smoke rose from Hickam Field after the Japanese bombed Pearl Harbor in Hawaii on December 7, 1941.

2,400 Americans died. The United States jumped fully into the war, and its warships and warplanes battled Japanese forces in the Pacific.

Nuclear research in the United States jolted into action. Money flooded into the race to build the world's first atomic bomb. In 1942 the Army asked physicist J. Robert Oppenheimer to find a way to use fission in a weapon. More than 130,000 people worked on the secret effort, which was named the Manhattan Project. In a specially designed laboratory in the mountains near Los Alamos, New Mexico, Oppenheimer gathered a team of gifted scientists. One of them, physicist Murray Peshkin, later recalled that "we were going to invent the weapon that would end this miserable war. And we did."

The scientists first needed to learn to control nuclear fission. In late 1942 physicist Enrico Fermi and other scientists stacked graphite blocks containing uranium inside a squash court under the University of Chicago

The world's first nuclear reactor was known as Chicago Pile-1.

"All of us ...
knew that
with the
advent of
the chain
reaction, the
world would
never be the
same again."

football stadium. Scientists watched with growing excitement as instruments registered neutrons bouncing wildly. Fissioning atoms spread heat through the pile like an invisible fire. The experiment proved that when enough uranium atoms are close together, they form a critical mass, and fission happens faster and produces more heat on its own. "All of us ... knew that with the advent of the chain reaction, the world would never be the same again," wrote physicist Samuel K. Allison.

A chain reaction of fission inside an atomic bomb's uranium takes less than a second, not slowly as in Fermi's 28-minute experiment. How did the Los Alamos scientists do it? By keeping the uranium separated until the last moment. Inside the tube-shaped bomb dropped on Hiroshima, a gunlike device shot one mass of uranium into another to produce a critical mass—the amount needed to make the chain reaction work. In the more powerful bomb dropped on Nagasaki, explosives fired at once, crushing the radioactive element plutonium into a critical mass.

At dawn on July 16, 1945, Los Alamos scientists got their first taste of their invention's power. The first atomic bomb exploded in a blinding, domed cloud that climbed 25,000 feet (7,620 m) above the New Mexico desert. Worry soon settled among the awestruck scientists. How was the bomb to be used?

They soon got their answer—the bombs were used to force Japan to surrender and thus end World War II. Yet the use of the bombs triggered another war, a 42-year "cold war." The Soviet Union tested its own atomic bomb in 1949. The race to make the first nuclear weapon had turned into a race to produce the largest number of them. No atomic bombs were dropped during the Cold War. Instead, the United States and the Soviet Union threatened each other with their ever-growing arsenals of weapons. Fear of nuclear destruction became part of many people's daily lives.

Yet nuclear energy also began to improve people's lives. Several years after the war, President Dwight D. Eisenhower encouraged people outside the military to use the hard-won knowledge of fission for peaceful purposes. Making electricity with fission became an exciting new field. Lewis Strauss, chairman of the U.S. Atomic Energy Commission, enthusiastically predicted that nuclear energy would make electricity cost almost nothing. "Our children will enjoy in their homes electrical energy too cheap to meter," he said.

How did scientists learn to use fission, which spikes the temperature inside an atomic bomb to 180 million F (100 million C), to power a plant like Fukushima Daiichi for decades at just 547 F (286 C)? Enrico Fermi, who is often called the father of the atomic bomb, also built the first nuclear reactor. In his 1942 experiment, he demonstrated how to control the speed of fission.

AN UNLUCKY BOAT

Japanese officials tested a tuna for radiation at a Tokyo fish market in March 1954. The tuna had been caught by the crew of the Lucky Dragon 5.

The crew of a Japanese fishing boat near the Marshall Islands saw the sky suddenly "painted in flaming sunset colors" on March 1, 1954. The United States was secretly testing atomic bombs on a Pacific island about 90 miles (145 km) away. When the 23 fishermen on the *Lucky Dragon 5* returned to Japan, they were hospitalized for radiation poisoning. One man died. The Japanese people were outraged at being victims of U.S. atomic weapons once again. After one-third of them signed antinuclear petitions, the government passed a law in 1955 forbidding use of nuclear energy except for peaceful purposes.

The U.S. was eager to repair the relationship with its new ally. After all, it had guided Japan in rebuilding itself after the war. Now it offered help with building a nuclear energy industry in Japan. President Eisenhower hoped to prove that the U.S. "wants to be constructive, not destructive." Through his "Atoms for Peace" program, the U.S. shared information with many countries about how to use nuclear energy, but not how to make nuclear weapons. Japanese citizens were hesitant, but the nation's leaders jumped at the opportunity. Japan's first nuclear power plant was under construction in the 1960s.

Fermi's team inserted rods of neutron-absorbing metals to slow or stop the fission process. When they removed the rods, fission resumed. Nuclear power plants still use control rods inside reactors to keep a steady temperature or to shut down fission, as they did in Fukushima Daiichi just after the earthquake.

Nuclear power created light in 1951, not as a fireball in the sky, but as four glowing light bulbs in Idaho. The Argonne National Laboratory built the world's first reactor to generate electricity. Four years later, a reactor used nuclear energy to bring electricity to the town of Arco, Idaho. The town of 1,300 people was the first to depend solely on nuclear power, although it was only for a two-hour experiment.

Nuclear power became a tempting new business opportunity. Making electricity by burning coal contributes to air pollution and global warming, is more expensive, and is less efficient than nuclear power generation. Fission using just one gram of uranium produces the same amount of electricity as 3 tons (2.7 metric tons) of coal or about 600 gallons (2,270 liters) of fuel oil. Eisenhower made sure the federal government shared information with the nuclear industry so "this greatest of destructive forces can be developed into a great boon for the benefit of all mankind."

Nuclear power not only brought electricity to homes, but it also was profitable. The first commercial nuclear plant in the world began making electricity in Cumbria,

Nuclear power plant cooling towers are a familiar sight around the world.

England, in 1956. It could produce enough electricity to power nearly 500,000 100-watt light bulbs. The next year, the first large nuclear plant began operating in Shippingport, Pennsylvania. Nuclear power plants grew larger and added reactors. A reactor at Fukushima Daiichi could generate enough electricity to power 37 million 100-watt light bulbs. Today 30 countries rely on 449 electricity generating reactors, and 60 more are under construction in 15 countries.

Chapter Three

A BRIGHT FUTURE

A dinosaur-like monster rose from the ocean less than a decade after atomic bombs fell on Japan. In 1954 millions of Japanese moviegoers watched *Gojira* crush buildings as wartime bombs had. Its destructive breath was hot and radioactive. Its rough skin suggested the scarred bodies of Hiroshima and Nagasaki survivors. Some audience members wept. The monster was unleashed by humans—nuclear testing had stirred it to life. "The moral was clear: nuclear war and the uncontrollable horrors within the atom were to be avoided at all cost," explained U.S. scholar William Tsutsui. (When a reimagined *Godzilla* movie reached U.S. audiences, references to the dangers of radioactivity and U.S. atomic testing had been removed.)

After the disaster of the Fukushima meltdowns in 2011, Japanese author Haruki Murakami was blunt. "This is a historic experience for us Japanese: our second massive nuclear disaster," he said. "But this time no one dropped a bomb on us. We set the stage, we committed the crime with our own hands, we are destroying our own lands, and we are destroying our own lives."

Why would the Japanese ever permit nuclear energy, in any form, onto its islands after its

"But this time no one dropped a bomb on us. We set the stage, we committed the crime with our own hands, we are destroying our own lands, and we are destroying our own lives."

Godzilla, the 1956 American movie starring Raymond Burr, was based on the Japanese *Gojira.*

traumatic history? The answer may lie with the occupants of a squadron of U.S. Navy ships that sailed into Tokyo harbor in 1853.

Centuries earlier foreign ships had been a
common sight around Japan. But the Japanese grew
frustrated with western traders and their attempts
to convert them to Catholicism. In 1639 Japan
closed its ports to nearly all westerners. When U.S.
Commodore Matthew Perry arrived nearly two

centuries later and boldly demanded that Japan open its port to the United States, the Japanese were impressed and intimidated by his well-armed, modern ships. They agreed to Perry's request.

Japan stepped closer to its future as a world power in 1868 when a group of warriors overthrew the government and established what would become a constitutional monarchy with Emperor Meiji as its figurehead. They imported technology and learning from the West while using Japanese history to create a new national identity.

Journalist and historian Tokutomi Soho wrote at the time that "the old Japan has already died, and what exists in the present day is the new Japan." The new Japan was modernizing. The Meiji government built railroads, shipyards, coal mines, and telephone systems. It pushed factories to produce steel, glass, cement, ammunition, and chemicals. The new Japan was hungry for territory and resources, such as coal. In 1894 it went to war with China. Over the next five decades, Japan fought Russia and took over Korea, the Philippines, and Burma (Myanmar).

Japan's defeat in World War II did not end its ambitions to be a global power. But the war's outcome meant it had to find new ways to achieve that status. Its factories churned out modern products the world craved. Japan exported cars, electronics, household appliances, and other goods. Panasonic, Sony, Canon,

Workers at a Honda factory in the late 1970s helped boost Japan's economy.

Toyota, Honda, Yamaha, and other companies brought wealth into Japan. By the 1980s Japan's economy had become the third largest in the world.

But Japan's lightning-quick progress depended on expensive imports. Japan's power plants needed more coal and oil to power factories and growing cities. With nuclear energy, Japan would only need to import small amounts of radioactive material for fuel. But the public was leery. The government and the electric power industry launched a campaign in the

The town of Futaba, with its pro-nuclear power banner, was deserted after the Fukushima disaster.

mid-1950s to sell the idea of a nuclear-powered Japan through traveling exhibits, films, and lectures. The town of Futaba, which was later evacuated during the Fukushima Daiichi disaster, adopted a new motto: "Nuclear power is the energy of a bright tomorrow."

Japan's first commercial nuclear power plant began generating electricity in 1966. Fukushima Daiichi's reactors—with their designs supplied by General Electric, Toshiba, and Hitachi—began operating in 1971. By the time the tsunami struck, more than 50 nuclear reactors were on Japan's shores, where seawater could cool hot pipes. They provided about 30 percent of Japan's electricity. By 1970 TEPCO was the world's largest privately owned utility.

The government paved the way for TEPCO's success. It rewarded rural communities that accepted construction of nuclear power plants with money and even new swimming pools and tennis courts. Since the mid-1970s, the government has poured $3.3 billion into the Fukushima prefecture, home to 10 TEPCO reactors. Still, people were wary. "Because there are risks, there is no way reactors would be built in Tokyo, but only here in this kind of rural area," said town official Shigenori Sasatake. But the government's offerings, and the promise of more jobs, made it hard to resist a new nuclear plant.

The government was supposed to monitor the nuclear industry. But its relationship with TEPCO was more of a partnership. People often moved between jobs as nuclear plant employees and jobs as government inspectors. So government inspectors doing safety checks at nuclear plants were often not strict. In 2002 TEPCO admitted that for years the company had lied about safety risks, including cracks inside 13 reactors. Five years later the company admitted to even more unreported safety

The government was supposed to monitor the nuclear industry. But its relationship with TEPCO was more of a partnership.

REMEMBERING CHERNOBYL

A memorial to the people who worked to contain the disaster and clean up its aftermath stands next to the abandoned Chernobyl nuclear plant.

Before the Fukushima nuclear disaster, there had been only one severe nuclear accident in the world. On April 26, 1986, a planned shutdown and systems tests at the Chernobyl nuclear power plant in Ukraine, then part of the Soviet Union, went terribly wrong. Workers had failed to follow safety guidelines. Flaws in the Soviet-designed reactors were revealed when a power surge caused an explosion in a reactor, and a fire burned for 10 days. About 10 times the amount of radiation released from Fukushima spread outside the Chernobyl plant and across Europe.

The Soviet government was slow to release information about the disaster to its people and the world. Eventually, though, the government relocated 335,000 people. In the months after the accident, at least 28 workers died from radiation exposure. Hundreds of thousands of workers brought in to clean up after the disaster were exposed to high levels of radiation, and many died. Today a 19-mile (30-km) exclusion zone encircles the abandoned plant.

Both Chernobyl and Fukushima earned level 7 ratings, the highest possible severity rating according to the International Atomic Energy Agency rating system. Level 7 indicates a major accident.

problems. The government simply trusted TEPCO to make the repairs. No inspectors visited the plant to make sure they were done.

Did this relaxed attitude toward safety put Fukushima Daiichi at risk? In 2002 government experts predicted there was a 20 percent chance of a dangerous tsunami during the next 30 years. In 2008 Fukushima Daiichi's own engineers warned that the plant's seawalls needed to be higher. But TEPCO took no action. Even so, just a month before the tsunami struck, the government had granted the plant permission to operate for another decade.

As news of the plant's disaster spread around the world, officials avoided sharing the whole story. TEPCO at first vaguely described the emergency as a "special event" at the plant. But company officials suspected it was much worse. Within the first three days after the disaster, loudspeakers at the plant announced that the "fuel has been exposed for some time now, so there is a possibility of a fuel meltdown." In fact, meltdowns were taking place in all three reactors. Yet TEPCO's president at the time, Masataka Shimizu, told employees to avoid the term "meltdown" and instead use the milder term "core damage" in public.

TEPCO "tried to make the disaster look small," said former government official Kenichi Matsumoto. On television, representatives of the government

A drone photographed the severely damaged nuclear plant a week after the tsunami hit.

encouraged people to remain calm without explaining the unfolding events. The U.S. Embassy in Japan warned Americans living in the area to stay 50 miles (80 km) away from the plant, more than four times the distance Japanese officials advised. Matsumoto, who was a special adviser to Japan's Cabinet at the

Reuters photographer Kim Kyung-Hoon wore protective gear inside the evacuation zone as he shot photos of the aftermath of the devastating earthquake and tsunami.

time of the earthquake and tsunami, admitted later that the government "knew right after the disaster that some people would not be able to live in their communities for 10 to 20 years. ... The government should have conveyed the truth to the evacuees. But it felt scared; it feared telling the truth to the people."

TEPCO did not allow journalists to enter Fukushima Daiichi for nearly a year. But Reuters photojournalist Kim Kyung-Hoon and others found ways to tell the story of the disaster. They visited areas smashed by tsunami waves or evacuated because of radiation fears. They photographed exhausted, grieving people in evacuation centers. Kyung-Hoon remembers most a frightened baby girl being checked for radiation exposure. He explained that turning his lens on people's suffering makes him uncomfortable, yet he feels a duty to bring the world's attention and help to the situation. To do their work, photojournalists must also face the same risks as their subjects. "Our white protective suits were mandatory to wear inside the evacuation zone," Kyung-Hoon explained. "I also stood in line to receive radiation screening with other evacuees at a radiation check-up point." He said "two palm-size radiation monitors" were added to his camera bag when he covered the Fukushima disaster.

The Fukushima Daiichi plant's employees were mostly on their own during the nine-month effort to stabilize the reactors. The government struggled with the aftermath of the deadly tsunami, and TEPCO watched from far-off Tokyo. But the workers were not resentful. "We were prepared to sacrifice everything," Yoshizawa later recalled. Japan has a long tradition of workers' feeling deep loyalty to the company that employs them. The only jobs Yoshizawa and Yoshida had ever had were at TEPCO. "It might seem strange to others, but it's natural for us to put our company

first," explained Yoshizawa. Yoshida's defiance of the order to stop spraying seawater, while unusual for a loyal employee, was appreciated—it saved TEPCO employees, Japan, and the world from a greater disaster. "I bow deeply out of respect for his leadership and decisiveness," said former Prime Minister Kan.

Fukushima Daiichi's workers do not call themselves heroes. They even feel some shame. Yoshizawa remembered finally leaving the plant with his coworkers, "stepping off that bus ... with long beards

Atsufumi Yoshizawa, one of the Fukushima 50

and disheveled hair, and each carrying a plastic bag containing a few possessions. But as we walked into the station no one gave us a second glance. Life in Tokyo appeared to be carrying on as normal, as if the Fukushima disaster had never happened. I sat down on the train and immediately noticed that people were avoiding sitting next to me." Yoshizawa explained that "generally speaking, people in Japan believe we were the cause of the accident, and it's important to bear that in mind. As TEPCO employees we have to take responsibility for the accident, and ensure that it never happens again. It's a matter of regaining people's trust, but it will take time."

Investigators in 2012 concluded that TEPCO, the government, and the regulators "effectively betrayed the nation's right to be safe from nuclear accidents." In 2016 three former TEPCO executives were charged in criminal court with contributing to the deaths and injuries caused by the triple meltdown at the power plant. A court ruled in 2017 that the government and TEPCO had failed to protect the public and bore responsibility for the disaster. The court said the disaster was "predictable" and that it was "possible to prevent the accident." The court ordered the government and TEPCO to pay damages to people who had been forced to evacuate. The ruling could influence many other lawsuits filed by disaster victims.

ChapterFour
DIFFICULT CHOICES

Sounds of construction filled the air along Japan's northeastern coast, where almost 250,000 people lost homes. Some towns rebuilt on higher ground. Others erected expensive seawalls. Japan's government in 2015 started lifting the evacuation order on some towns near the plant so residents could move back. In fact, no death has yet been blamed directly on the radiation released by the triple meltdown. In more good news, the World Health Organization has determined that the disaster should not endanger the future health of people in towns near the plant. But the cancer risk for workers inside the plant during the early days of the disaster is elevated.

An eerie silence filled some towns near the plant. There were open schoolbooks on desks, dirty dishes in sinks, and laundry in washing machines. All were left during the evacuation and have gathered years of dust. The radiation is still too high for people to live in the 12-mile (20-km) exclusion zone. Pets that were left behind run wild in packs, and radioactive wild boars roam through abandoned homes. In 2011 about 150,000 people fled the radiation danger, and few have returned. "In war, nuclear weapons destroy everything in a moment," said Yuji Onuma, who was evacuated from a town 5 miles (8 km) from the

A radiation monitor in front of a damaged house about 11 miles (18 km) from the plant indicated higher than normal amounts of radiation one month after the disaster.

Fukushima plant. "In the case of a nuclear power plant accident, people are deprived of everything in a moment. So it is the same thing."

The wind spread the most radioactive contamination northwest in a narrow path stretching about 25 miles (40 km) across Fukushima prefecture. In a clean-up effort estimated to cost $188 billion, tens of thousands of workers in protective gear use simple tools to remove surfaces where radioactive material settled. They scoop

away topsoil and grind away concrete surfaces.
More than 10 million black plastic bags filled with
radioactive debris line roads and fill fields and
valleys. But these areas may still have radiation doses
10 times the acceptable levels. And heavily forested
areas cannot be cleaned at all. Evacuee Onuma said
he accepts that things will never be the same as they
were. "This is our reality," he said. "It is what it is and
we can't change it."

Many people who evacuated are not planning
to return home. An elderly evacuee explained that
"most young people simply won't go back. They

Japan's Ministry of the Environment estimated in 2017 that it has bagged 3.5 billion gallons of contaminated soil. It plans to collect much more.

fear for their children, but also they have moved on in their lives, with new jobs and their children in new schools." Yet Prime Minister Shinzo Abe said that the "government is resolved to fully lift the evacuation orders [in the no-go zones], even if it takes a long time." After being misled by TEPCO and government officials during the disaster, many still mistrust their advice. Government officials "have every incentive to downplay the level of risk and to put a positive spin on it," suggested Tokyo-based professor Kyle Cleveland.

More than 6,000 people are working at the epicenter of the nuclear disaster. Much has changed at Fukushima Daiichi since 2011. After the meltdown, the government assumed control of TEPCO, since the company could not afford to clean up the affected area and compensate evacuees. The government claims that radiation levels in the seawater outside the plant are as safe as those in drinking water. And they say that radiation at the plant is so low that workers no longer wear protective gear in most areas. But this pleasant image could be an illusion. In February 2017 radiation inside unit 2 measured seven times as high as readings in 2012. And research by a Woods Hole Oceanographic Institution scientist indicates that it still seeps into the Pacific Ocean.

Experts predict it will take decades to bring this nuclear disaster under control. Workers could simply encase the radioactive cores with concrete and steel, as was done at Chernobyl. But a Japanese government report pointed out that "the uncertainties over passing down responsibilities for a long period of time and concerns over easy postponement from one generation to another" must be considered. TEPCO manager Yuichi Okamura explained simply, "We promised the local people that we would recover the site and make it a safe ground again."

Water continues to play both the hero and the villain of Fukushima Daiichi's story. Rain and melted snow in the nearby Abukuma Mountains flow down through an underground layer of porous rocks. Each day thousands of gallons of groundwater pour into the plant's basements, where it mixes with radioactive water used for cooling reactors. Engineers tried blocking groundwater with an underground ice wall. Pumps keep contaminated water from overflowing into the ocean by moving it into tanks 95 feet (29 m) tall. But the more than 818,000 tons (742,077 metric tons) of stored radioactive water makes nuclear experts like Dale Klein uneasy. The TEPCO adviser and former chairman of the U.S. Nuclear Regulatory Commission said, "I get nervous about just storing all that water when you have about a thousand tanks. You have all the piping, all the valves, everything that can break." Engineers are experimenting with treating stored water to eliminate all radioactivity so it can be released into the ocean.

ROBOT EXPLORERS

Robots have rolled over debris and climbed stairs inside Fukushima Daiichi's reactor buildings. Cameras captured images and sensors measured temperature and radiation. But in the first few years after the disaster, TEPCO workers had to guess at what exactly happened inside the reactors. Radiation there can spike high enough to kill a human within minutes of exposure. Engineers have struggled to design robots that can survive risky missions to locate melted fuel.

A 2-foot (61-cm) snakelike robot slithered into a reactor in 2015 but stalled before completing its mission. Engineers lost more robots, including one with a flexible, scorpion-like tail equipped with a camera. The robots got stuck or intense radiation destroyed their electronics.

Engineers' determination has finally paid off. In early 2017 a remote-controlled camera took blurry images of possible clumps of melted fuel. It helped answer a question workers had asked since March 11, 2011: Had the fuel nearly escaped to open air? The answer was yes. It probably melted through the container's steel layer and fell onto the concrete layer's floor. In July 2017 an underwater robot the size of a bread loaf that was nicknamed the "Little

An underwater robot examined contaminated water within the plant.

Sunfish" finally gave engineers a clear, close-up view of the nuclear disaster. The robot turned 180 degrees to record the damaged reactor's interior. In ghostly light it showed melted fuel hanging like icicles from control rods.

Once engineers have mapped the locations of all melted fuel, they will form a plan and start removing it, most likely after the 2020 Tokyo Olympics.

Workers viewed a monitor screen to check the removal of a nuclear fuel rod in 2014.

TEPCO must clean up the source of Fukushima Daiichi's problems—radioactive fuel. Workers began removing used fuel rods in 2014. But removing melted nuclear fuel from inside three reactors is a delicate and dangerous task. It will not be completed until at least 2050, TEPCO officials predict.

Beyond the nuclear reactors, another source of radiation terrified people in Fukushima prefecture and beyond. Shortly after the nuclear disaster, people in Fukushima prefecture wore masks to filter radiation in the air. But how could they filter radiation out of food before they put it in their mouths? People feared that crops, even tea leaves, were radioactive because radiation fell with the rain into soil. They worried about milk from cows that had eaten contaminated grass. They worried about seafood caught in radioactive seawater. Government officials tested seafood more strictly than almost anywhere in the world. Researchers took almost a million samples of foods to test, especially for the long-lived radioactive isotope cesium-137. Before food could head to market, its radiation had to be shown to not exceed Japan's limit, which was one-sixth of Europe's limit. Experts agree that almost no harmful food ever made it to tables.

Despite this success, some of the disaster's consequences have no clear solutions. Shame has haunted those who were involved in the accident. When Japan's prime minister first publicly thanked the workers who saved the plant—more than 18 months after the accident—the men refused to be photographed or to give their names. TEPCO did not want them to tell their story and embarrass the company. The workers also wanted to protect their families from blame and harassment. Sometimes evacuated children were bullied at their new schools. They were called "radioactive" and told to "go back to Fukushima!"

Nuclear electrical generation is controversial across Japan. A newspaper survey in late 2016 found

Former Prime Minister Naoto Kan spoke against nuclear energy at a March 11, 2017, rally in Tokyo. It marked the sixth anniversary of the earthquake and tsunami that devastated Japan.

that 57 percent of the public opposed restarting nuclear power plants and 73 percent favored a complete phaseout of nuclear power. Even Naoto Kan became an antinuclear advocate after leaving the prime minister's office. People protested when the government began restarting nuclear reactors after they were shut down in May 2011 for extensive safety checks. Even as electricity bills rose during the shutdown, polls showed that people were still firmly opposed to nuclear energy. This antinuclear attitude affects how people vote and what political candidates talk about in their campaigns.

Yet Japan's government and business leaders have never given up on nuclear electrical generation. Every year since 1960, a nuclear reactor has been under construction somewhere in Japan. On the Fukushima disaster's five-year anniversary, Prime Minister Shinzo Abe said, "Our resource-poor country cannot do without nuclear power." Engineers have not given up either. They have developed ways to keep nuclear fuel cool without electricity. For example, tanks release gravity-driven water that can keep nuclear fuel cool for days. And reactor cores are immersed in liquid sodium, which absorbs a tremendous amount of heat without boiling away.

The United States also tolerates nuclear electrical generation despite a level 5 disaster at Three Mile Island in 1979. Twenty-three of the country's 99 reactors even share a similar design to Fukushima Daiichi's. In March 2011 President Barack Obama spoke with concern about Japan's unfolding nuclear disaster, but he also reminded Americans that "here at home, nuclear power is also an important part of our own energy future." He said that "when we see a crisis like the one in Japan, we have a responsibility to learn from this event, and to draw from those lessons to ensure the safety and security of our people."

The Fukushima disaster did drive some countries away from nuclear electrical generation. France plans to reduce its dependence on nuclear power from 75 percent of its energy needs to 50 percent by 2025. Just months after the Fukushima accident, Germany announced plans to close all nuclear plants by 2022. "I think we're on a good path but very, very many questions have to be considered," said German Chancellor Angela Merkel. A critical one is what can replace the power of the atom?

Wind or flowing water can spin turbines, and solar panels can capture the sun's energy to make electricity. Renewable energy advocates say about a half million wind turbines filling an area the size of Rhode Island could supply the United States with all of its electrical needs. Solar panels covering an area smaller than West Virginia could do the same job, they say. Japan's leaders hope renewable energy will provide almost a quarter of the country's energy needs by 2030. To that end, the country has experimented with floating beds of solar panels and offshore wind turbines anchored to the seafloor.

The double disaster at Fukushima Daiichi will long be remembered. "Mankind has never faced the forces of physics and the forces of nature that those people faced," said U.S. nuclear expert Chuck Casto, a former member of the Nuclear Regulatory Commission, which regulates American nuclear plants. Nuclear engineer Atsufumi Yoshizawa admitted, "I don't kid myself that life will ever be the same." Today Yoshizawa helps

"Mankind has never faced the forces of physics and the forces of nature that those people faced."

Farmers who refused a government order to kill their cows care for them as part of a research project. Scientists check on the cows every three months.

manage the process of dismantling the plant safely. The disaster forced many Japanese to start new lives in new places. It drove some to join protests against nuclear power. It inspired some to invest in companies making electricity in safer ways.

It even inspired a few to feed abandoned cows living in Fukushima's exclusion zone. At first their efforts were out of love for the cows, but now university scientists study them to learn more about how radiation can affect people. The survivors all hope the world never forgets the Fukushima disaster. Evacuee Yuji Onuma said, "We want the world to learn from what we're going through here."

Timeline

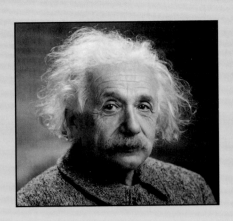

1905

Scientist Albert Einstein proposes the theory that matter can become energy

1938

German scientists Otto Hahn and Fritz Strassmann and Austrian scientist Lise Meitner demonstrate nuclear fission through an experiment and mathematical analysis

1951

Argonne National Laboratory's nuclear reactor in Idaho becomes the world's first to produce electricity

1953

President Eisenhower introduces the "Atoms for Peace" program

1942

Physicist Enrico Fermi's experiments demonstrate the first nuclear fission chain reaction

1945

The United States drops the first atomic bombs on Japan to end World War II

1954

The crew of the *Lucky Dragon 5* is poisoned by U.S. atomic testing in the Pacific Ocean, motivating the United States to help Japan start its nuclear electrical generation program

1966

The first nuclear reactor in Japan begins operations

Timeline

1971

Fukushima Daiichi starts operations

1979

An accident at Three Mile Island, the worst such event at a commercial U.S. nuclear electrical generation plant, prompts the government to improve emergency procedures for nuclear accidents

1986

An accident at Ukraine's Chernobyl nuclear plant, the worst nuclear plant disaster in world history, prompts mass evacuations and causes radiation-related deaths and sickness

2014

All used fuel rods are removed from Fukushima Daiichi storage pools

2015

Protests erupt when Japan restarts a nuclear reactor for the first time since the Fukushima disaster

2002

TEPCO admits to falsifying safety records at its nuclear plants

2011

An earthquake and tsunami on March 11 trigger a triple meltdown at Fukushima Daiichi

2012

The Japanese government takes control of TEPCO as the company slides toward bankruptcy

2016

Three former TEPCO executives are charged with contributing to the deaths and injuries caused by the Fukushima accident

2017

A Japanese court rules that the government and TEPCO failed to protect the public and bore responsibility for the Fukushima disaster

Glossary

atom—smallest unit of a chemical element; atoms contain electrons, protons, and neutrons

compensation—award, usually of money, to make up for loss or damage

electron—negatively charged particle that whirls around the nucleus of an atom

exclusion zone—area into which entry is forbidden

genetic—relating to physical traits or conditions passed down from parents to children

millisievert—unit used to measure radiation exposure

neutron—particle in the nucleus of an atom that has no electric charge

nucleus—dense core of an atom that contains protons and neutrons

physics—science that studies matter, energy, force, and motion

prefecture—an area into which some countries are divided; Japan has 47 prefectures

proton—positively charged particle in the nucleus of an atom

renewable—not depleted when used

Additional Resources

Further Reading

Bortz, Fred. *Meltdown!: The Nuclear Disaster in Japan and Our Energy Future.* Minneapolis: Twenty-First Century Books, 2012.

Conkling, Winifred. *Radioactive!: How Irène Curie and Lise Meitner Revolutionized Science and Changed the World.* Chapel Hill, N.C.: Algonquin Young Readers, 2016.

Owen, Ruth. *Energy from Atoms: Nuclear Power.* New York: PowerKids Press, 2013.

Rissman, Rebecca. *Swept Away: The Story of the 2011 Japanese Tsunami.* North Mankato, Minn.: Capstone Press, 2017.

Internet Sites

Use FactHound to find Internet sites related to this book.
Visit *www.facthound.com*
Just type in 9780756557423 and go.

Critical Thinking Questions

Do you think the close relationship between TEPCO and the Japanese government was more helpful or harmful to Japan? Use examples from the text to support your answer.

Studies show that radiation released by the Fukushima disaster did not significantly threaten people's health. Yet the disaster affected many people in many ways. Consider plant workers and managers, government and TEPCO officials, evacuees, people living outside the evacuation zone, and people around the world. Explain how various groups suffered for various reasons. Which group or groups of people do you think faced the greatest challenges and why?

Look closely at TEPCO's choice of words when discussing the Fukushima disaster in public. How did they use language to shape public opinion?

Source Notes

Page 6, line 13: Justin McCurry. "Fukushima 50: 'We felt like kamikaze pilots ready to sacrifice everything.'" *The Guardian*. 11 Jan. 2013. 19 Sept. 2017. https://www.theguardian.com/environment/2013/jan/11/fukushima-50-kamikaze-pilots-sacrifice

Page 7, line 9: Ari Beser. "Exclusive: One Man's Harrowing Story of Surviving the Japan Tsunami." Fulbright National Geographic Stories. *National Geographic*. 23 March 2016. 19 Sept. 2017. http://voices.nationalgeographic.com/2016/03/23/exclusive-one-mans-harrowing-story-of-surviving-the-japan-tsunami/

Page 8, line 1: David McNeill. "'I am one of the Fukushima fifty:' One of the men who risked their lives to prevent a catastrophe shares his story." *The Independent*. 2 March 2013. 19 Sept. 2017. http://www.independent.co.uk/news/world/asia/i-am-one-of-the-fukushima-fifty-one-of-the-men-who-risked-their-lives-to-prevent-a-catastrophe-8517394.html

Page 9, line 1: "Nuclear Meltdown Disaster 2015." *NOVA*. PBS. 8 April 2016. 19 Sept. 2017. https://www.youtube.com/watch?v=A20_JGZ71-o

Page 9, line 19: Ibid.

Page 10, line 14: "Inside Japan's Nuclear Meltdown." *Frontline*. PBS. 28 Feb. 2012. 19 Sept. 2017. http://www.pbs.org/video/frontline-inside-japans-nuclear-meltdown/

Page 11, col. 1, line 2: Miles O'Brien. "The heroes of Fukushima Dai-ichi, but don't call them that." *PBS Newshour*. PBS. 13 March 2016. 19 Sept. 2017. http://www.pbs.org/newshour/updates/the-heroes-of-fukushima-daiichi-but-dont-call-them-that/

Page 11, col. 2, line 10: Mari Shibata. "After Fukushima disaster, Japanese mothers don lab coats to measure radiation." Reuters. 8 March 2017. 19 Sept. 2017. http://uk.reuters.com/article/japan-women-radiation-idUKL8N1G66K0

Page 12, line 1: Kim Kyung-Hoon. "Japan's nuclear crisis and my life." Photographers' Blog. Reuters. 13 April 2011. 19 Sept. 2017. http://blogs.reuters.com/photographers-blog/2011/04/13/japans-nuclear-crisis-and-my-life/

Page 14, line 10: Norimitsu Onishi and Martin Fackler. "In Nuclear Crisis, Crippling Mistrust." *The New York Times*. 12 June 2011. 19 Sept. 2017. http://www.nytimes.com/2011/06/13/world/asia/13japan.html?hp=&pagewanted=print

Page 14, line 19: Hiroko Tabuchi. "Masao Yoshida, Nuclear Engineer and Chief at Fukushima Plant, Dies at 58." *The New York Times*. 9 July 2013. 19 Sept. 2017. http://www.nytimes.com/2013/07/10/world/asia/masao-yoshida-nuclear-engineer-and-chief-at-fukushima-plant-dies-at-58.html

Page 15, line 3: "Nuclear Meltdown Disaster 2015."

Page 15, line 12: "Fukushima 50: 'We felt like kamikaze pilots ready to sacrifice everything.'"

Page 16, line 7: Hiroko Tabuchi. "Videos Shed Light on Chaos at Fukushima as a Nuclear Crisis Unfolded." *The New York Times*. 9 Aug. 2012. 19 Sept. 2017. http://www.nytimes.com/2012/08/10/world/asia/fukushima-videos-shed-light-on-chaos-in-nuclear-crisis.html

Page 16, line 14: "Nuclear Meltdown Disaster 2015."

Page 16, line 19: "Masao Yoshida, Nuclear Engineer and Chief at Fukushima Plant, Dies at 58."

Page 16, line 23: Justin McCurry. "Japanese government held liable for first time for negligence in Fukushima." *The Guardian*. 17 March 2017. 19 Sept. 2017. https://www.theguardian.com/world/2017/mar/17/japanese-government-liable-negligence-fukushima-daiichi-nuclear-disaster

Page 18, line 12: Vibeke Venema. "When time stood still: A Hiroshima survivor's story." BBC News. 24 July 2014. 19 Sept. 2017. http://www.bbc.co.uk/news/special/2014/newsspec_8079/index.html

Page 18, line 18: Justin McCurry. "The man who survived Hiroshima: 'I had entered a living hell on earth.'" *The Guardian*. 3 Aug. 2015. 19 Sept. 2017. https://www.theguardian.com/world/2015/jul/31/japan-atomic-bomb-survivors-nuclear-weapons-hiroshima-70th-anniversary

Page 20, line 1: Transmitted by Domei and Recorded by the Federal Communications Commission. "Emperor Hirohito, Accepting the Potsdam Declaration, Radio Broadcast." 14 August 1945. 19 Sept. 2017. Documents of World War II. Mount Holyoke College. https://www.mtholyoke.edu/acad/intrel/hirohito.htm

Page 22, line 3: "Einstein Letter." Archives. Franklin D. Roosevelt Presidential Library and Museum. 19 Sept. 2017. http://www.fdrlibrary.marist.edu/archives/pdfs/docsworldwar.pdf

Page 22, line 24: Alan Taylor. "World War II: Pearl Harbor." World War II in Photos. *The Atlantic*. 31 July 2011. 19 Sept. 2017. https://www.theatlantic.com/photo/2011/07/world-war-ii-pearl-harbor/100117/

Page 24, line 6: "Voices of the Manhattan Project." *The New York Times*. 28 Oct. 2008. 19 Sept. 2017. http://www.nytimes.com/interactive/2008/10/28/science/28manhattanproject.html?ref=science&_r=0

Page 25, line 8: Steve Koppes. "How the first chain reaction changed science: Legacy of 1942 breakthrough on campus includes advances in many fields." 19 Sept. 2017. The University of Chicago. http://www.uchicago.edu/features/how_the_first_chain_reaction_changed_science/

Page 26, line 20: Cutler Cleveland and Christopher Morris, eds. *Handbook of Energy. Volume I*. Boston: Elsevier, 2014, p. 186.

Page 27, col. 1, line 2: Mark Schreiber. "Lucky Dragon's Lethal Catch." *The Japan Times*. 18 March 2012. 19 Sept. 2017. http://www.japantimes.co.jp/life/2012/03/18/general/lucky-dragons-lethal-catch/

Page 27, col. 2, line 5: James W. Feldman, ed. *Nuclear Reactions: Documenting American Encounters with Nuclear Energy*. Seattle: University of Washington Press, 2017, p. 76.

Page 28, line 23: Jesse Hicks. "Atoms for Peace: The Mixed Legacy of Eisenhower's Nuclear Gambit." *Distillations*. Summer 2014. 19 Sept. 2017. Chemical Heritage Foundation. https://www.chemheritage.org/distillations/magazine/atoms-for-peace-the-mixed-legacy-of-eisenhower%E2%80%99s-nuclear-gambit

Page 30, line 9: Tsutsui, William. *Godzilla on My Mind: Fifty Years of the King of Monsters*. New York: Palgrave Macmillan, 2004, p. 33.

Page 30, line 18: Craig Nelson. *The Age of Radiance: The Epic Rise and Dramatic Fall of the Atomic Era*. New York: Scribner, 2014, p. 359.

Page 33, line 13: Helen Hardacre and Adam L. Kern, eds. *New Directions in the Study of Meiji Japan*. New York: Brill, 1997, p. 12.

Page 35, line 5: Craig Nelson. "'The Energy of a Bright Tomorrow:' The Rise of Nuclear Power in Japan." *Origins*. Vol. 4, Issue 9. June 2011. 19 Sept. 2017. http://origins.osu.edu/article/energy-bright-tomorrow-rise-nuclear-power-japan

Page 36, line 13: Martin Fackler and Norimitsu Onishi. "In Japan, a Culture That Promotes Nuclear Dependency." *The New York Times*. 30 May 2011. 19 Sept. 2017. http://www.nytimes.com/2011/05/31/world/asia/31japan.html

Page 38, line 16: "Nuclear Meltdown Disaster 2015."

Page 38, line 19: "Videos Shed Light on Chaos at Fukushima as a Nuclear Crisis Unfolded."

Page 38, line 24: Claire Bernish. "Coverup of Fukushima Meltdown by Japanese Government in Concert with TEPCO." Global Research. Centre for Research on Globalization. 27 June 2016. 20 Sept. 2017. http://www.globalresearch.ca/coverup-of-fukushima-meltdown-by-japanese-government-in-concert-with-tepco/5532967

Page 38, line 26: Mark Willacy. "Japan 'scared' of telling truth to Fukushima evacuees." Australian Broadcasting Corporation. 28 Sept. 2011. 19 Sept. 2017. http://www.abc.net.au/news/2011-09-28/fukushima-residents-unable-to-return-home/3026496

Page 40, line 2: Ibid.

Page 41, line 11: "Japan's nuclear crisis and my life."

Page 41, line 23: "Fukushima 50: 'We felt like kamikaze pilots ready to sacrifice everything.'"

Page 41, line 27: "'I am one of the Fukushima fifty:' One of the men who risked their lives to prevent a catastrophe shares his story."

Page 42, line 5: Justin McCurry. "Fukushima boss hailed as hero dies." *The Guardian*. 10 July 2013. 19 Sept. 2017. https://www.theguardian.com/world/2013/jul/10/fukushima-plant-boss-hero-dies

Page 42, line 10: "Fukushima 50: 'We felt like kamikaze pilots ready to sacrifice everything.'"

Page 43, line 8: Ibid.

Page 43, line 15: "Japanese government held liable for first time for negligence in Fukushima."

Page 43, line 23: Motoko Rich. "Japanese Government and Utility Are Found Negligent in Nuclear Disaster. *The New York Times*. 17 March 2017. 19 Sept. 2017. https://www.nytimes.com/2017/03/17/world/asia/japan-fukushima-nuclear-disaster-tepco-ruling.html

Page 44, line 23: Christina Nunez. "Frozen Clocks and Radiation Mark Fukushima's Abandoned Towns." *National Geographic*. 10 March 2017. 19 Sept. 2017. http://news.nationalgeographic.com/2017/03/fukushima-nuclear-disaster-exclusion-zone-anniversary/

Page 46, line 8: "An Eerie Look Inside Japan's Nuclear Exclusion Zone." *National Geographic*. 10 March 2017. 20 Sept. 2017. http://video.nationalgeographic.com/video/news/170310-fukushima-exclusion-zone-vin 2:35

Page 46, line 12: Fred Pearce. "In Fukushima, a Bitter Legacy of Radiation, Trauma and Fear." Yale Environment 360. 19 March 2016. 20 Sept. 2017. http://e360.yale.edu/features/fukushima_bitter_legacy_of_radiation_trauma_fear

Page 47, line 4: "Evacuation orders lifted for three more Fukushima areas but residents slow to return." *The Japan Times*. 31 March 2017. 20 Sept. 2017. http://www.japantimes.co.jp/news/2017/03/31/national/evacuation-orders-lifted-three-fukushima-areas-residents-slow-return/#.WQrCdfl96M-

Page 47, line 8: Motoko Rich. "The Children of Fukushima Return, Six Years After the Nuclear Disaster." *The New York Times*. 21 April 2017. 20 Sept. 2017. https://www.nytimes.com/2017/04/21/world/asia/japan-fukushima-nuclear-disaster-children.html?_r=0

Page 48, line 2: "'Stone coffin' eyed for decommissioning Fukushima plant: report." *The Mainichi*. 14 July 2016. 20 Sept. 2017. http://mainichi.jp/english/articles/20160714/p2a/00m/0na/009000c

Page 48, line 6: Motoko Rich. "Struggling With Japan's Nuclear Waste, Six Years After Disaster." *The New York Times*. 11 March 2017. 20 Sept. 2017. https://www.nytimes.com/2017/03/11/world/asia/struggling-with-japans-nuclear-waste-six-years-after-disaster.html?_r=1

Page 48, line 23: Stephen Stapczynski and Emi Urabe. "Treated Fukushima Water Safe for Release, Tepco Adviser Says." *Bloomberg News*. 5 Sept. 2016. 20 Sept. 2017. https://www.bloomberg.com/news/articles/2016-09-05/treated-fukushima-water-safe-for-release-tepco-adviser-says

Page 51, line 25: Mizuho Aoki. "Survey finds bullying against young Fukushima evacuees in schools." *The Japan Times*. 11 April 2017. 20 Sept. 2017. http://www.japantimes.co.jp/news/2017/04/11/national/social-issues/survey-finds-bullying-young-fukushima-evacuees-schools/#.WQrTmPl96M8

Page 53, line 6: "Shinzo Abe says Japan 'cannot do without' nuclear power, on eve of Fukushima disaster." *South China Morning Post*. 11 March 2016. 20 Sept. 2017. http://www.scmp.com/news/asia/east-asia/article/1922953/shinzo-abe-says-japan-cannot-do-without-nuclear-power-eve

Page 53, line 21: "Obama's Speech on Japan." *The New York Times*. 17 March 2011. 20 Sept. 2017. http://www.nytimes.com/2011/03/17/us/politics/18obama-japan-text.html

Page 54, line 5: "Germany: Nuclear power plants to close by 2022." BBC News. 30 May 2011. 20 Sept. 2017. http://www.bbc.com/news/world-europe-13592208

Page 54, line 22: "Nuclear Meltdown Disaster 2015."

Page 54, line 27: "Fukushima 50: 'We felt like kamikaze pilots ready to sacrifice everything.'"

Page 55, line 12: "An Eerie Look Inside Japan's Nuclear Exclusion Zone."

Select Bibliography

Cleveland, Cutler, and Christopher Morris, eds. *Handbook of Energy. Vol. I.* Boston: Elsevier, 2014.

"Einstein Letter." Archives. Franklin D. Roosevelt Presidential Library and Museum. 19 Sept. 2017. http://www.fdrlibrary.marist.edu/archives/pdfs/docsworldwar.pdf

Fackler, Martin. "Japanese Coastal Town Still Struggling to Rebuild from 2011 Tsunami." *The New York Times.* 12 March 2015. 20 Sept. 2017. https://www.nytimes.com/2015/03/13/world/asia/japanese-coastal-town-still-struggling-to-rebuild-from-2011-tsunami.html?_r=0

Feldman, James W., ed. *Nuclear Reactions: Documenting American Encounters with Nuclear Energy.* Seattle: University of Washington Press, 2017.

"Fukushima Accident." World Nuclear Association. September 2017. 5 Oct. 2017. http://www.world-nuclear.org/information-library/safety-and-security/safety-of-plants/fukushima-accident.aspx

"Fukushima Daiichi: ANS Committee Report." American Nuclear Society. June 2012. 20 Sept. 2017. http://fukushima.ans.org/report/Fukushima_report.pdf

"Fukushima Site Still Leaking After Five Years, Research Shows." Woods Hole Oceanographic Institution. 7 March 2016. 6 Oct. 2017. http://www.whoi.edu/news-release/fukushima-site-still-leaking

"Fukushima Timeline." *Scientific American.* 19 Sept. 2017. https://www.scientificamerican.com/media/multimedia/0312-fukushima-timeline/#1

Hardacre, Helen, and Adam L. Kern, eds. *New Directions in the Study of Meiji Japan.* New York: Brill, 1997.

Iwata, Masakuzu. *Ōkubo Toshimichi: The Bismarck of Japan.* Berkeley: University of California Press, 1964.

"Japan's Modern History: An Outline of the Period." Asia for Educators. Columbia University. 20 Sept. 2017. http://afe.easia.columbia.edu/timelines/japan_modern_timeline.htm

Jha, Alok. "E=mc2: Einstein's equation that gave birth to the atom bomb. *The Guardian.* 5 April 2014. 20 Sept. 2017. https://www.theguardian.com/science/2014/apr/05/einstein-equation-emc2-special-relativity-alok-jha

Kyung-Hoon, Kim. "Japan's nuclear crisis and my life." Photographers' Blog. Reuters. 13 April 2011. 19 Sept. 2017. http://blogs.reuters.com/photographers-blog/2011/04/13/japans-nuclear-crisis-and-my-life/

Lochbaum, David A., Edwin Lyman, Susan Q. Stranahan and The Union of Concerned Scientists. *Fukushima: The Story of a Nuclear Disaster.* New York: The New Press, 2014.

Martin, Tim. "Godzilla: Why the Japanese original is no joke." *The Telegraph.* 15 May 2014. 20 Sept. 2017. http://www.telegraph.co.uk/culture/film/10788996/Godzilla-why-the-Japanese-original-is-no-joke.html

McMahon, David. "Fukushima's organic farmers still battle stigma." *The Japan Times.* 18 March 2016. 20 Sept. 2017. http://www.japantimes.co.jp/life/2016/03/18/food/fukushimas-organic-farmers-still-battle-stigma/

"Meet the Fukushima 50? No, you can't." *The Economist.* 8 Oct. 2012. 20 Sept. 2017. https://www.economist.com/blogs/banyan/2012/10/japans-nuclear-disaster

"The Meiji Restoration and Modernization." Asia for Educators. Columbia University. 20 Sept. 2017. http://afe.easia.columbia.edu/special/japan_1750_meiji.htm

Nelson, Craig. *The Age of Radiance: The Epic Rise and Dramatic Fall of the Atomic Era.* New York: Scribner, 2014.

"Nuclear Power in Japan." World Nuclear Association. August 2017. 20 Sept. 2017. http://www.world-nuclear.org/information-library/country-profiles/countries-g-n/japan-nuclear-power.aspx

"Reference Data for RFI." International Research Institute for Nuclear Decommissioning. September 2017. http://irid.or.jp/debris/Reference_E.pdf

Sample, Ian. "Japan earthquake and tsunami: what happened and why." *The Guardian.* 11 March 2011. 20 Sept. 2017. https://www.theguardian.com/world/2011/mar/11/japan-earthquake-tsunami-questions-answers

Sim, M. "Radiation 101: What is it, how much is dangerous, and how does Fukushima compare to Chernobyl?" Pollution Blog. Pure Earth. 6 April 2011. 20 Sept. 2017. http://www.pureearth.org/blog/radiation-101-what-is-it-how-much-is-dangerous-and-how-does-fukushima-compare-to-chernobyl/

Sovacool, Benjamin K., and Scott Victor Valentine. *The National Politics of Nuclear Power: Economics, Security, and Governance.* New York: Routledge, 2012.

"Summary of the Atomic Energy Act." U.S. Environmental Protection Agency. 19 Sept. 2017. https://www.epa.gov/laws-regulations/summary-atomic-energy-act

Suzuki, Tatsujiro. "6 Years after Fukushima, Japan's Energy Plans Remain Murky." The Conversation. *Scientific American.* 15 March 2017. 20 Sept. 2017. https://www.scientificamerican.com/article/6-years-after-fukushima-japans-energy-plans-remain-murky1/

Transmitted by Domei and Recorded by the Federal Communications Commission. "Emperor Hirohito, Accepting the Potsdam Declaration, Radio Broadcast." 14 August 1945. Documents of World War II. Mount Holyoke College. 19 Sept. 2017. https://www.mtholyoke.edu/acad/intrel/hirohito.htm

Tsutsui, William. *Godzilla on My Mind: Fifty Years of the King of Monsters.* New York: Palgrave Macmillan, 2004.

"The United States and the Opening to Japan, 1853." Milestones: 1830-1860. Office of the Historian. Department of State. 20 Sept. 2017. https://history.state.gov/milestones/1830-1860/opening-to-japan

Vastag, Brian, Rick Maese and David A. Fahrenthold. "U.S. Urges Americans within 50 miles of Japanese nuclear plant to evacuate; NRC chief outlines dangerous situation." *The Washington Post.* 16 March 2011. 20 Sept. 2017. https://www.washingtonpost.com/national/us-urges-americans-within-50-miles-of-japanese-nuclear-plant-to-evacuate/2011/03/16/ABwTmha_story.html?utm_term=.4aa7d095613e

"Voices of the Manhattan Project." *The New York Times.* 28 Oct. 2008. 19 Sept. 2017. http://www.nytimes.com/interactive/2008/10/28/science/28manhattanproject.html?ref=science&_r=0

Index

About the Author

As a teacher, Danielle Smith-Llera taught children to think and write about literature before writing books for them herself. As the spouse of a diplomat, she enjoys living in both Washington, D.C., and overseas in countries such as India, Jamaica, and Romania.